ALVIN JAMES II

Credit Unlocked: Zero to Prosperity

Building Wealth and Freedom Through Credit Mastery

First edition

This book was professionally typeset on Reedsy.
Find out more at reedsy.com

Contents

1

Chapter 1.The Power of Credit:

My name is Alvin James and I was 18, a freshman in college when I first heard about the concept of credit. I was 18 when I first heard about credit. Back then, it was just a mysterious concept adults discussed—a number that could supposedly make or break your future. It wasn't until I started diving into financial literacy that I realized credit wasn't just a number; it was a tool. A tool that could open doors to endless opportunities I never thought possible. In the coming chapter, I'm I will going to break down what credit is, why it's vital for financial success, and how it can transform your life—just like it did mine.

What is Credit?

At its core, credit is simple: it's the ability to borrow money or access goods and services with the promise to pay for them later. Whether it's a loan from a bank, a swipe of a credit card, or financing a car, credit is the bridge between where you are now and where you want to be financially. But here's the thing: credit is much more than borrowed money. It's a reflection of trust—trust that you will pay back what you owe. And this trust is quantified into what we know as a credit score.

Let's Break It Down:

Credit Score: A three-digit number (ranging from 300 to 850) that tells lenders how trustworthy you are when it comes to handling money. A higher score means you're a safer bet.

Credit Report: Think of this as your financial report card. It shows all your borrowing activity—loans, credit cards, on-time payments, and even mistakes like late payments or defaults.

Types of Credit:

Revolving Credit: Think credit cards—money you can borrow, repay, and borrow again.

Installment Credit: Loans like car payments or mortgages, repaid in fixed amounts over time.

Open Credit: Agreements where you pay in full, like utility bills.

When I was just starting out, I couldn't fully grasp the power of these concepts. But as I began to educate myself, I came to realize that credit wasn't just about buying things I was unable to afford at a given moment. It was about building a foundation for financial success.

Why is Credit a Vital Tool for Financial Success

Let me be transparent with you, fully grasping and understanding the concept of credit has become a game-changer in my life. I'll be honest: credit has been a game-changer in my life. It's Utilizing credit in the correct manner is he reason I've been able to secure over $50,000 in business credit by the age of 22. The source that has allowed me to start up multiple businesses of my own, even contributing to my mother's launch of her own. It's the reason I've started multiple businesses and even helped my mom launch hers. Credit is not just a tool, it is a lifeline. Here's why:

Access to Capital for Investments:

Credit allowed me to invest in opportunities I never could have afforded upfront. Whether it was starting a business, buying essential equipment, or funding marketing campaigns, credit gave me the capital

2

to take action. For entrepreneurs like me, credit is the lifeblood of growth.

Building Wealth:

Strategic credit use can help you acquire assets that grow in value over time. For example, leveraging credit for real estate investments or a business venture can yield exponential returns. In my case, I used credit to fund businesses that now generate steady income streams.

Emergency Preparedness:

Life is unpredictable, and emergencies happen. Credit provides a safety net, whether it's a medical emergency, a car repair, or an unexpected expense. Having access to funds during those critical moments is invaluable.

Establishing Financial Credibility:

A strong credit score isn't just about loans and credit cards. It impacts your ability to rent an apartment, secure low-interest rates, and even get a job in some industries. Credit is your financial reputation.

Scaling Opportunities:

Once I built a strong credit profile, I unlocked larger credit limits and access to business funding. This allowed me to scale my ventures and reinvest profits into bigger opportunities.

Improved Financial Options:

Good credit gives you access to the best financial products—low-interest loans, premium credit cards with rewards, and better mortgage rates. In short, it saves you money while giving you more flexibility.

The Pitfalls of Mismanaged Credit

While credit has been my biggest ally, it can also become your biggest enemy if you don't manage it wisely. Here are a few lessons I've learned along the way:

Debt Overload: Spending beyond your means can lead to a cycle of debt that's hard to escape.

High-Interest Costs: Carrying balances on high-interest credit cards can drain your finances.

Damaged Credit: Late payments or defaults can tank your credit score, making it harder to access opportunities in the future.

The key is to use credit as a tool, not a crutch. It's not free money—it's borrowed money that must be repaid responsibly.

Credit as a Tool, Not a Crutch

Here's the most important thing I want you to take away from this chapter: credit isn't just a number. It's a pathway to financial freedom, but only if you treat it with respect. By maintaining low utilization, paying bills on time, and using credit strategically, you can turn it into a powerful tool for building the life you've always wanted.

Credit changed my life. At 22, I've been able to achieve financial milestones that many people don't hit until their 30s or 40s. And if I can do it, so can you.

This book is your guide to unlocking the power of credit. By the end of this journey, you'll not only understand how credit works, but you'll also know how to use it to create opportunities, build wealth, and transform your life.

Let's unlock your potential—one credit move at a time.

This sets a strong foundation for your book while keeping the content engaging, educational, and relatable. Let me know if you'd like to add or adjust anything!

2

Chapter 2: The Journey to a 750+ Credit Score at 22:

Whel people I have a 750+ credit score at the age of 22, they're often surprised. Some think it's luck, others think I must have had help. But the truth is, it wasn't easy, and it didn't happen overnight. My journey to building a strong credit score began with a simple job at Lowe's and a commitment to discipline and education.

Starting at Lowe's: My First Steps Toward Financial Freedom

At 20, I started working at Lowe's, earning a steady paycheck for the first time. Like many young adults, I had financial responsibilities but no real knowledge of credit. All I knew was that I wanted more for my future, and I realized that I needed to educate myself about money management.

Working at Lowe's gave me the stability I needed to make my first big financial decision: applying for a credit card. It wasn't anything flashy—just a basic card with a modest limit. But for me, it was the beginning of something much bigger.

Building My Credit with Personal Credit Cards

I treated my first credit card with the utmost respect. I didn't see it as a way to buy things I couldn't afford but as a tool to build trust with lenders. Every purchase was intentional, and I followed a few simple rules that would lay the foundation for my 750+ credit score:

1. Keep Utilization Low:

I made sure never to use more than 30% of my credit limit at any given time. If my limit was $1,000, I'd only spend up to $300 before paying it down.

1. Pay on Time, Every Time:

Late payments weren't an option. I set reminders for due dates and made sure to pay off my balance in full whenever possible. This one habit alone accounted for a significant portion of my credit score growth.

1. Use Credit for Everyday Expenses:

I used my credit card for things I was already buying—groceries, gas, and occasional small purchases. This way, I wasn't creating new debt; I was simply shifting my spending.

1. Avoid Overapplying:

I knew every credit inquiry could hurt my score, so I avoided applying for multiple cards at once. I was strategic and only applied when it made sense.

Discipline Over Time

For two years, I worked diligently to build my credit profile. Every paycheck I earned at Lowe's was partially dedicated to paying down my credit card balances. I avoided impulse spending and stayed focused on my long-term goals.

During this time, I also began educating myself about the nuances of credit scores. I learned about the five key factors that determine your score:

1. Payment History (35%): Always pay on time.

2. Credit Utilization (30%): Keep balances low.

3. Credit History Length (15%): Start early and keep accounts open.

4. **Credit Mix (10%): Maintain a mix of credit types (e.g., credit cards, loans).

5. New Credit (10%): Avoid too many inquiries.

Understanding these factors helped me stay intentional about every financial decision I made. By the time I turned 22, my credit score had climbed to an impressive 750+. But I wasn't done yet—I wanted to leverage that score to create something bigger.

Leveraging Credit to Qualify for Business Funding

Building my credit was only the first step. I knew that to achieve my entrepreneurial dreams, I needed access to capital. That's where business funding came into play.

Here's how I transitioned from personal credit to securing over $50,000 in business credit:

1. Set Up an LLC:

I registered my first business, laying the groundwork for legitimacy. This step was critical because most lenders want to see a formal business structure before they offer funding.

2. Leverage Personal Credit as a Guarantor:

When you're just starting out, many lenders require a personal guarantee for business credit. My strong personal credit score made me an ideal candidate for approval.

3. Apply for Business Credit Cards:

Using my personal credit as leverage, I applied for business credit cards with high limits. These cards gave me the flexibility to invest in equipment, marketing, and other essentials for my ventures.

4. Strategic Use of Funds:

I didn't squander the credit I secured. Every dollar went toward building my businesses and generating returns. This discipline ensured that I could pay back the borrowed funds without falling into debt.

The Results: A Life Transformed

By the time I finished leveraging my personal credit for business funding, I had secured over $50,000 in capital. This money allowed me to:

Start multiple businesses, including ventures that continue to generate income today.

Help my mom launch her own business, something I'm incredibly proud of.

Build a sense of financial independence and security that many people my age don't yet have.

None of this would have been possible without those two years of discipline and intentional credit-building. Working at Lowe's may have been my starting point, but the habits I developed during that time became the foundation for my financial success.

Lessons Learned Along the Way

1. Patience Pays Off:

Building a strong credit score doesn't happen overnight. It requires consistent effort and discipline.

2. Knowledge is Power:

Understanding how credit works gave me the confidence to use it strategically. I wasn't guessing; I was executing a plan.

3. Leverage Wisely:

Credit isn't just about spending—it's about creating opportunities. When used correctly, it can be a powerful tool for growth.

At 22, I've achieved financial milestones that many people don't reach until much later in life. This is only the beginning for me. In the next chapter, I'll take you deeper into the strategies underwriters look for when approving applications, so you yourself can replicate my success and unlock your own financial potential.

This chapter not only shares your journey but also sets up readers for actionable takeaways. Let me know if you'd like any edits!

3

Chapter 3: What Underwriters Look For

When I first started applying for business credit, I thought approval was all about luck or who you knew. After digging deeper, I came to the realization that there is a science to getting approved. Lenders and underwriters don't randomly decide whether to trust you—they follow a specific formula. Once you understand what they're looking for, you can position yourself to get automatic approvals, just like I did. In this chapter, I'll break down the key factors that underwriters examine when reviewing your credit applications and show you how to align your profile to secure funding.

What Are Underwriters?

Underwriters are the decision-makers behind the scenes. They're the ones who assess your creditworthiness and decide if you're a good candidate for a loan or credit line. Their job is to minimize risk for lenders by analyzing specific financial metrics.

Think of underwriters as gatekeepers: if you meet their criteria, they'll open the door to approval. If not, they'll close it, and you're left wondering why.

The good news? Underwriters don't make decisions based on feelings—they rely on data. That means you can prepare yourself to meet their expectations.

The Key Factors Underwriters Look For

Here are the primary elements that underwriters assess and how you can optimize each one:

1. Low Credit Inquiries

What It Means: A credit inquiry occurs when you apply for a loan or credit card. Too many inquiries in a short period can make you look desperate for credit, which is a red flag for underwriters.

What You Should Do:

Limit your applications to one or two every six months.

Be strategic about which credit products you apply for. Research the qualifications beforehand to ensure you're a strong candidate.

2. Low Credit Utilization

What It Means: Credit utilization is the percentage of your available credit that you're currently using. Underwriters prefer to see a utilization rate of 30% or less.

What You Should Do:

- Pay down your balances before applying for new credit.

- Request a credit limit increase on your cards to lower your utilization rate (but don't use the extra credit for unnecessary spending).

- Spread your spending across multiple cards to avoid maxing out any single account.

3. Revolving Credit

- What It Means: Revolving credit, like credit cards, shows underwriters that you can responsibly manage borrowed money. Having a mix of revolving accounts in good standing demonstrates financial reliability.

- What You Should Do:

- Keep your revolving accounts active and in good standing.

- Avoid closing older credit cards, as they contribute to your credit history length.

4. Payment History

- What It Means: Your payment history is the single most significant factor in your credit score. Late or missed payments are major red flags for underwriters.
- What You Should Do:
- Automate your payments to ensure you never miss a due date.
- If you've missed payments in the past, focus on building a consistent on-time payment streak moving forward.

5. Length of Credit History

- What It Means: The longer your credit history, the more data underwriters have to assess your reliability. A short credit history can make you seem like a risk.
- What You Should Do:
- Start building credit as early as possible.
- Keep your oldest accounts open, even if you don't use them frequently.

The Automation Secret: Triggering Approvals Instantly

One of the most valuable lessons I have learned is how to optimize my credit profile to trigger automatic approvals. Many lenders use algorithms to make approval decisions without human intervention. If your profile aligns with their criteria, you can get approved in seconds. Here's how to position yourself:

1. Align Your Credit Utilization: Keep your utilization under 10% for maximum impact. If your total credit limit is $10,000, aim to use less than $1,000 at any given time.

2. Maintain a Perfect Payment Record: Even one late payment can derail your chances. Set up auto-pay for all your accounts to eliminate this risk.

3. Ensure a Strong Credit Mix: Underwriters favor applicants with a balance of revolving credit (credit cards) and installment loans (like car loans or personal loans). If you don't have a mix, consider responsibly

adding another type of credit to your profile.

4. Minimize Hard Inquiries: Before applying for a loan or card, check if the issuer offers pre-qualification tools. These tools allow you to see your likelihood of approval without affecting your credit score.

My Experience: The Day I Got Approved

I remember the first time I applied for a business credit card, spending months I spent months fine-tuning my credit profile. I made sure my utilization was low, my payment history was spotless, and my inquiries were minimal. When I hit the submit button, I held my breath.

A few seconds later, I saw the words: "You're Approved!"

That single moment validated all the hard work and discipline I had put into my credit journey. It wasn't luck—it was preparation. I knew what the underwriters were looking for, and I delivered exactly that.

The Power of Preparation

Understanding what underwriters look for puts the power back in your hands. Instead of blindly applying for credit and hoping for the best, you can approach every application with confidence, knowing that you've aligned your profile with their expectations. With the right preparation, you can unlock doors that once seemed out of reach, just like I did.

4

Chapter 4: Setting Up an LLC: The Step-by-Step Guide to Starting Your LLC

W hen I first decided to pursue business credit, one thing became crystal clear: having a registered business entity was essential. Lenders aren't just looking for individuals with strong credit—they're looking for legitimate businesses they can trust. That's where forming a Limited Liability Company (LLC) comes in.

In this chapter, I'll walk you through the steps to form your own LLC, explain why this structure is ideal for entrepreneurs, and show you how it connects to accessing business funding.

What is an LLC and Why is It Important?

A Limited Liability Company (LLC) is a type of business structure that provides personal liability protection while offering flexibility in how the business is taxed. Essentially, it separates your personal assets from your business, which is crucial for protecting your financial future.

Why an LLC Matters:

1. Credibility: Registering an LLC makes your business look more professional to lenders, clients, and investors.

2. Liability Protection: If your business faces financial trouble, your personal assets (like your home or car) are shielded from business debts.

3. Access to Business Credit: Most lenders require a formal business entity before they'll extend credit. An LLC creates the foundation you need to qualify for business funding.

Step-by-Step Guide to Forming an LLC

Forming an LLC may sound complicated, but it's simpler than you think. Follow these steps, and you'll have your business entity up and running in no time.

Step 1: Choose Your Business Name

- Tips for Choosing a Name:

- Make it unique: Check your state's database to ensure the name isn't already taken.

- Reflect your brand: Choose a name that aligns with your business's vision and services.

- Avoid restricted words: Some words (like "Bank" or "Insurance") may require additional approvals.

Step 2: Register Your Business Name (Optional)

- If you plan to operate under a different name than your LLC (a "Doing Business As" or DBA), you'll need to register that name with your state.

Step 3: Choose a Registered Agent

- A Registered Agent is a person or company designated to receive official documents, like tax forms or legal notices, on behalf of your LLC.

- Requirements for a Registered Agent:

- Must have a physical address in the state where your LLC is registered.

- Must be available during business hours.

You can be your own Registered Agent, but hiring a professional service can save you time and ensure compliance.

Step 4: File Articles of Organization
- The Articles of Organization is the document that officially creates your LLC.
- What You'll Need to Include:
- LLC name and address.
- Registered Agent information.
- Names of the owners (members) of the LLC.
- Where to File: Submit this form to your state's Secretary of State office. Many states allow online filing.
- Cost: Filing fees range from $50 to $500, depending on your state.

Step 5: Create an Operating Agreement (Optional but Recommended)
- An Operating Agreement outlines how your LLC will be managed. While not always required, it's a good idea to have one, especially if you have multiple members in your LLC.
- Key Elements to Include:
- Ownership percentages.
- Roles and responsibilities of each member.
- Procedures for decision-making and conflict resolution.

Step 6: Get an Employer Identification Number (EIN)
- An EIN is like a Social Security Number for your business. You'll need it to open a business bank account, apply for business credit, and file taxes.

How to Get an EIN: Apply for free on the IRS website. It takes just a few minutes.

Step 7: Open a Business Bank Account
- Once your LLC is registered, open a dedicated business bank account. This step is critical for separating your personal and business finances.
- Why It's Important:

- Helps you track business income and expenses.
- Build credibility with lenders.
- Ensures compliance with tax laws.

How LLCs Connect to Business Funding

Forming an LLC isn't just about looking professional—it's about positioning yourself for financial growth. Here's how having an LLC directly impacts your ability to access business funding:

1. Legitimacy to Lenders:
- When you apply for business credit, lenders want to see that you're running a legitimate operation. An LLC provides the structure and documentation they need to trust you.

2. Access to Business Credit Cards:
- With your EIN and business bank account, you can apply for business credit cards. These cards often come with higher limits, better rewards, and 0% APR introductory offers—perfect for funding business expenses.

3. Separation of Finances:
- Having a clear distinction between personal and business finances makes you more attractive to lenders. It also simplifies tax filing and protects your personal assets.

4. Opportunities for Growth:
- Many business loans and grants require applicants to have a registered business entity. Without an LLC, you're limiting your options for growth.

5. Building Business Credit:
- An LLC allows you to start building a business credit profile, separate from your personal credit. Over time, this profile will open doors to larger funding opportunities.

Real-Life Application: My First LLC

When I started my first LLC, I was nervous. It felt like such a big step, and I wasn't sure if I was ready. But once I completed the process,

I realized how much credibility it gave me. Suddenly, I wasn't just a guy with an idea—I was the owner of a legitimate business. That LLC became the foundation for everything that followed, from securing business credit cards to funding my entrepreneurial ventures.

Common Mistakes to Avoid

1. Skipping the Operating Agreement: Even if you're the sole owner, an Operating Agreement can prevent future misunderstandings and show lenders you're serious about your business.

2. Using Your Personal Bank Account: Mixing personal and business finances is a major red flag for lenders and can lead to tax complications.

3. Failing to Renew Your LLC: Many states require annual filings or fees to keep your LLC active. Stay on top of these requirements to avoid penalties.

Action Steps for You

- Decide on your business name and check its availability.
- File your Articles of Organization with your state.
- Obtain your EIN and open a business bank account.
- Start tracking your business income and expenses.
- Begin applying for business credit cards or small loans to build your business credit profile.

Forming an LLC is one of the most important steps you'll take as an entrepreneur. It's more than just paperwork—it's a declaration that you're serious about your vision. With your LLC in place, you're ready to take the next step: leveraging your business entity and personal credit to secure funding that will fuel your dreams.

Chapter 5: Leveraging Credit for Business: Achieve Financial Freedom

O nce I had my LLC and my personal credit score in place, the next step was figuring out how to use these tools to fuel my business dreams. This is where everything came together—leveraging the credit I had worked so hard to build to create opportunities that transformed my life.

In this chapter, I'll show you exactly how to use personal and business credit strategically to grow your business, fund new ventures, and take your first steps toward financial freedom.

Why Leverage Credit for Business Growth?

Using credit isn't about taking on unnecessary debt—it's about using borrowed capital to invest in opportunities that will generate returns. Done right, leveraging credit allows you to:

- Expand your business operations.
- Purchase essential equipment or inventory.
- Invest in marketing to reach more customers.

- Scale faster than you could with just personal savings.

The key is using credit strategically, ensuring every dollar borrowed is part of a bigger plan for growth.

Step 1: Securing Business Credit

The first step in leveraging credit for business growth is accessing the right type of credit. Here's how to do it:

1. Business Credit Cards:
   - Once your LLC is set up, you can apply for business credit cards. These cards often come with higher limits, better rewards, and 0% APR introductory offers—perfect for managing short-term expenses.
   - How I Used It: My first business credit card helped me fund a marketing campaign that brought in enough new customers to pay off the balance and turn a profit.

2. Vendor and Supplier Credit:
   - Many suppliers offer credit terms, allowing you to purchase inventory or services upfront and pay later. This helps you manage cash flow and invest in growth without draining your bank account.
   - Example: Partnering with vendors who offer Net-30 or Net-60 payment terms can give you time to generate revenue before payment is due.

3. Small Business Loans:
   - For larger expenses, consider applying for a small business loan. Your personal credit score and LLC will be critical in securing these funds.
   - Pro Tip: Look for loans with low interest rates and repayment terms

that align with your cash flow projections.

Step 2: Creating a Plan for Your Credit

Before spending a dime of borrowed money, it's essential to have a plan. Credit is a tool, but without a strategy, it can quickly become a liability.

Steps to Create Your Credit Plan:
1. Define Your Goals:
- What will you use the credit for? Examples include purchasing equipment, hiring staff, or launching a new product.
2. Set a Budget:
- Determine how much funding you need and how it will be allocated.
3. Estimate ROI:
- Every dollar borrowed should generate a return. Calculate how your investment will translate into revenue or cost savings.
4. Track Your Spending:
- Use accounting software or hire a bookkeeper to monitor expenses and ensure you stay within budget.

My Example: When I started my first business, I used a portion of my credit to purchase inventory. I calculated the profit margin on each product and ensured that my sales would cover the credit payments while leaving me with a profit.

Step 3: Managing and Paying Off Business Credit

Credit is powerful, but it comes with responsibility. Properly managing your credit ensures you maintain a strong profile and avoid financial trouble.

Best Practices for Managing Business Credit:

1. Pay on Time:
- Set up automatic payments to avoid missing due dates.
2. Avoid Overutilization:
- Just like with personal credit, keep your business credit utilization below 30%.
3. Reinvest Wisely:
- Use profits from your investments to pay off balances and reinvest in the business.

Pro Tip: Take advantage of rewards programs offered by business credit cards. Many offer cashback, travel points, or discounts on business-related purchases, which can help you save money over time.

Step 4: Leveraging Credit for Growth

Here's where the magic happens. Once you've secured and managed your credit, it's time to use it to scale your business.

1. Expand Operations:
- Use credit to invest in resources that allow you to serve more customers. For example, hire additional staff, upgrade equipment, or open a new location.
2. Marketing and Advertising:
- Invest in strategies to increase brand awareness and drive sales. Credit can help you fund social media ads, email campaigns, or promotional events.
3. Diversify Your Offerings:
- Credit can fund the development of new products or services, allowing you to tap into new markets.

My Example: I used a portion of my business credit to hire a professional web designer. The improved website boosted my online sales, allowing me to recoup the investment within a few months.

Mistakes to Avoid When Leveraging Credit

While credit is a powerful tool, it can also be dangerous if mismanaged. Avoid these common pitfalls:

1. Overborrowing: Don't take on more credit than you can reasonably repay.
2. Failing to Track Spending: Losing track of expenses can lead to overspending and debt.
3. Using Credit for Non-Essential Purchases: Only use credit for expenses that directly contribute to your business goals.

My Journey: Leveraging Credit for Multiple Ventures

By the age of 22, I had used personal and business credit to launch multiple ventures. Here's what I have learned along the way:

- Start Small: My first use of business credit was a small investment in inventory. The profits from that investment allowed me to scale gradually.
- Diversify: Once I gained confidence, I used credit to fund other ventures, including helping my mom start her own business. Seeing her succeed was one of the most rewarding parts of my journey.
- Stay Disciplined: Every credit decision was part of a bigger plan. I avoided impulse spending and focused on long-term growth.

Action Steps for You

1. Evaluate Your Credit Readiness: Ensure your personal credit score and LLC are in good standing.

2. Research Funding Options: Look into business credit cards, vendor credit, and small business loans.

3. Create a Credit Plan: Define your goals, set a budget, and calculate ROI before borrowing.

4. Take Action: Use credit strategically to invest in opportunities that will grow your business.

Leveraging credit has been the key to my financial transformation. It's allowed me to take risks, seize opportunities, and create a life of freedom and success. But remember, credit is a tool—it's up to you to use it wisely.

6

Chapter 6: Avoiding Credit Pitfalls

Credit can be a powerful tool, but like any tool, it must be used with care. Throughout my journey, I've seen people make mistakes with personal and business credit that set them back years financially. The good news is that with the right knowledge and strategies, these mistakes can be avoided—or even repaired.

In this chapter, we'll discuss the most common pitfalls people face with credit and explore proven strategies for managing debt and repairing damaged credit.

Common Mistakes People Make with Credit

1. Overutilization of Credit

- What It Is: Using a high percentage of your available credit, often over 30% of your credit limit.

- Why It's a Problem: High utilization lowers your credit score and signals to lenders that you may be financially overextended.

- How to Avoid It:

- Keep your balances below 30% of your total credit limit.

- Pay down balances before your statement date to reduce reported utilization.

2. Late Payments

- What It Is: Missing the due date on your credit card or loan payments.
- Why It's a Problem: Payment history accounts for 35% of your credit score. Even one missed payment can significantly lower your score.
- How to Avoid It:
- Set up automatic payments or calendar reminders.
- Pay at least the minimum due, even if you can't pay in full.

3. Opening Too Many Accounts at Once
- What It Is: Applying for multiple credit cards or loans in a short period, leading to several hard inquiries on your credit report.
- Why It's a Problem: Too many inquiries can lower your credit score and make you appear desperate for credit.
- How to Avoid It:
- Be strategic about applying for credit. Only apply when you truly need it.
- Use pre-qualification tools that don't affect your credit score.

4. Mixing Personal and Business Credit
- What It Is: Using personal credit cards for business expenses or vice versa.
- Why It's a Problem: This blurs the line between personal and business finances, making it harder to track expenses and manage debt.
- How to Avoid It:
- Open separate accounts for personal and business use.
- Use business credit cards or loans exclusively for business-related expenses.

5. Ignoring Credit Reports
- What It Is: Failing to regularly review your credit reports for errors or fraudulent activity.
- Why It's a Problem: Errors on your report can hurt your credit score, and identity theft can go unnoticed.
- How to Avoid It:

- Check your credit reports annually through [AnnualCreditReport.c om](https://www.annualcreditreport.com).
- Dispute any inaccuracies with the credit bureaus immediately.

Strategies for Debt Management

If you've accumulated debt, don't panic! Managing and paying off debt is possible with a clear plan and disciplined execution. Here are some effective strategies:

1. The Debt Snowball Method
- Focus on paying off your smallest debt first while making minimum payments on larger debts.
- Once the smallest debt is paid off, move to the next smallest, creating momentum.

2. The Debt Avalanche Method
- Focus on paying off the debt with the highest interest rate first, minimizing the total amount of interest paid over time.

3. Consolidate Debt
- Consider consolidating high-interest debts into a single loan with a lower interest rate. This simplifies payments and can save money on interest.

4. Create a Budget
- Track your income and expenses to identify areas where you can cut back and allocate more money toward debt repayment.

5. Negotiate with Creditors
- If you're struggling to make payments, reach out to your creditors. Many are willing to offer temporary relief, such as lower interest rates or payment plans.

Strategies for Credit Repair

If your credit has taken a hit, it's not the end of the road. Here's how you can repair your credit and rebuild trust with lenders:

1. Pay Down Balances
- Reducing your credit utilization is one of the fastest ways to improve your credit score. Focus on paying off high balances first.
2. Dispute Errors
- Review your credit report for inaccuracies, such as incorrect account balances or late payments. File disputes with the credit bureaus to correct these errors.
3. Build a Positive Payment History
- Start making on-time payments consistently, even if it's just the minimum. Over time, this will rebuild your payment history.
4. Use a Secured Credit Card
- If your credit score is too low to qualify for traditional credit cards, consider a secured credit card. Use it responsibly to build a positive credit history.
5. Limit Hard Inquiries
- Avoid applying for new credit while repairing your score. Each hard inquiry can temporarily lower your score.
6. Become an Authorized User
- Ask a trusted family member or friend to add you as an authorized user on their credit card. Their positive payment history can help boost your score.
7. Monitor Your Credit
- Use credit monitoring services to track your progress and receive alerts for any changes to your report.

My Experience with Debt Management and Credit Repair

I haven't always been perfect with credit. Early on, I made mistakes like carrying balances too high and opening accounts without a clear plan. I quickly realized that owning my mistakes and implementing strategies, like the Debt Snowball Method and strict budgeting, helped me turn things around.

One key moment was disputing an error on my credit report. A lender had incorrectly reported a late payment, and I immediately filed a dispute with the credit bureau. Within a month, the error was corrected, and my score rebounded.

How to Stay on Track

The best way to avoid credit pitfalls is to stay proactive. Here are some habits that will keep your credit healthy:

- Regularly review your credit reports.
- Keep your utilization low and pay balances in full when possible.
- Educate yourself about credit and stay updated on best practices.

Action Steps for You

1. Review your credit reports for errors and dispute any inaccuracies.

2. Choose a debt repayment strategy (Snowball or Avalanche) and create a plan.

3. Commit to paying at least the minimum due on time each month.

4. Avoid applying for new credit while working on repairs.

5. Celebrate small wins along the way to stay motivated.

Mistakes with credit are not the end of the road—they're lessons. By learning from them and implementing the strategies in this chapter, you can regain control of your financial future.

Chapter 7: Scaling Your Business Dreams

S ecuring funding and starting your business is just the beginning. The real magic happens when you take the profits from your ventures and reinvest them into opportunities that allow you to scale. Reinvestment is the key to long-term growth and financial independence. In this chapter, I'll walk you through how to strategically reinvest your profits to expand your business, create new income streams, and maximize your return on investment.

Why Reinvesting is Crucial

Reinvesting profits is about thinking long-term. It's easy to get excited about early success and spend your profits on personal luxuries, but short-term thinking can limit your business's potential. Here's why reinvestment matters:

1. Fuel for Growth:

- Profits provide the resources to hire more staff, invest in better equipment, or scale your operations to meet growing demand.

2. Building Momentum:

- Consistent reinvestment creates a snowball effect. Each round of growth builds on the last, leading to exponential results.

3. Diversification:
   - Reinvesting allows you to explore new opportunities, reducing your reliance on a single income stream.

4. Financial Security:
   - By growing your business, you're creating a stronger financial foundation for the future.

Step 1: Assess Your Profits

Before reinvesting, you need to understand your profits and where they're coming from. Here's how to evaluate your financial position:

1. Calculate Net Profit:
   - Subtract your total expenses (including funding repayments) from your total revenue. The remaining amount is your net profit.

2. Identify Profit Drivers:
   - What products or services are generating the most profit? Focus on reinvesting in areas with high returns.

3. Set Aside Savings:
   - Always set aside a portion of your profits for emergencies or unexpected expenses. Aim for at least 10–20% of your profits.

Step 2: Create a Reinvestment Plan

Once you know your profits, it's time to create a reinvestment plan. A clear strategy ensures your money is spent effectively.

1. Define Your Goals:

   - Do you want to increase production capacity? Expand your customer base? Launch a new product? Your reinvestment plan should align with your business goals.

2. Allocate Funds:

   - Break down your profits into specific categories, such as marketing, equipment upgrades, and staff training.

3. Set Timelines:

   - Establish a timeline for your reinvestment activities to ensure you stay on track.

Example: When I reinvested my first round of profits, I allocated 40% to marketing, 30% to inventory, and 20% to upgrade my website. The remaining 10% went into savings.

Step 3: Focus on Scalable Opportunities

Reinvesting in scalable opportunities ensures that each dollar spent generates a higher return over time. Here are some areas to consider:

1. Marketing and Advertising

   - Investing in targeted marketing campaigns can help you reach more customers and increase revenue.
   - Pro Tip: Focus on digital marketing channels like social media ads, email marketing, and search engine optimization (SEO). They offer high returns on investment.

2. Technology and Automation
  - Upgrade your technology to streamline operations and improve efficiency. For example, investing in customer relationship management (CRM) software can help you manage leads and sales more effectively.
  - Automating repetitive tasks allows you to focus on strategic growth.

3. Expanding Product or Service Offerings
  - Use profits to develop new products or services that align with your brand. This diversifies your income streams and attracts new customers.

4. Team Development
  - Hire skilled employees or invest in training programs for your team. A strong, capable team is essential for scaling your business.

5. Geographic Expansion
  - Consider expanding into new markets or opening additional locations to increase your reach.

6. Building Reserves for Larger Investments
  - Set aside funds for significant future opportunities, such as real estate, major equipment purchases, or large-scale marketing initiatives.
  Step 4: Measure and Adjust

Reinvestment is an ongoing process. To ensure success, you need to monitor your investments and make adjustments as needed.

1. Track ROI:
  - Measure the return on investment for each reinvestment activity. For example, if you spend $1,000 on marketing, track how much revenue that campaign generates.

2. Analyze Results:
   - Evaluate what worked and what didn't. Focus future reinvestments on areas with the highest returns.

3. Stay Flexible:
   - Business needs evolve, so be prepared to adjust your reinvestment plan as new opportunities arise.

Example: After investing in social media ads, I realized that Instagram generated the most engagement and sales. I shifted more of my budget toward that platform, maximizing my results.

Real-Life Application: My Reinvestment Journey

When I started my first business, I used the profits to reinvest in areas that directly impacted growth. For example:
   - Marketing: I launched a social media campaign that doubled my customer base in three months.
   - Inventory: I used profits to purchase more inventory at bulk rates, increasing my profit margins.
   - Technology: Upgrading my website improved customer experience and boosted online sales.

Each reinvestment decision was part of a larger plan to scale my business. Over time, these small steps add up to significant growth.

Common Mistakes to Avoid

1. Reinvesting Without a Plan:
   Spontaneous spending can lead to wasted resources. Always have a clear strategy.

2. Ignoring Cash Flow:

Ensure you have enough cash on hand for daily operations before reinvesting.

3. Overinvesting in Low-Yield Areas:

- Focus on activities that generate the highest returns, rather than spreading your funds too thin.

Action Steps for You

1. Calculate your profits and identify high-performing areas of your business.

2. Create a detailed reinvestment plan with specific goals and timelines.

3. Focus your reinvestments on scalable opportunities like marketing, technology, and team development.

4. Monitor your results and adjust your strategy to maximize ROI.

Reinvesting profits is how you turn a small venture into a thriving business. It's a process of disciplined decision-making and long-term thinking. By using the strategies in this chapter, you'll be well on your way to scaling your business and creating financial freedom.

8

Chapter 8: Your Roadmap to Financial Freedom

Now that you've reached the end, you have a wealth of knowledge about credit, business funding, and strategies for building financial freedom. It's important to remember that knowledge alone won't create results—it's the action you take that transforms your life. In this chapter, I'll outline practical steps you can take immediately to start leveraging credit, launching your business, and achieving your financial goals.

Step 1: Assess Your Current Financial Position

Before you can move forward, you need to know where you stand. Take the following steps to evaluate your personal and financial situation:

1. Check Your Credit Report and Score:
   - Use [AnnualCreditReport.com](https://www.annualcreditreport.com) to get a free copy of your credit report.
   - Look for any errors or inaccuracies and dispute them if necessary.

- Note your credit score and identify areas for improvement.

2. List Your Debts:
   - Write down all your outstanding debts, including credit card balances, loans, and payment amounts.

3. Determine Your Available Credit:
   - Calculate your total credit limit and current utilization rate. Aim to keep utilization below 30%.

Step 2: Set Clear Financial Goals

Clarity is the foundation of progress. Define specific, measurable goals to guide your next steps. Examples include:
   - Improving your credit score by 50 points in six months.
   - Securing your first business credit card within three months.
   - Launching an LLC within 30 days.

Pro Tip: Break your goals into smaller milestones to make them manageable and track your progress along the way.

Step 3: Start Building or Repairing Credit

Whether you're starting from scratch or recovering from past mistakes, take steps to strengthen your credit profile:

1. Pay Down Balances:
   - Focus on reducing high credit utilization to boost your score quickly.

2. Make On-Time Payments:
   - Automate payments to avoid missed due dates.

3. Use a Secured Credit Card:
   - If your credit score is low, apply for a secured credit card and use it responsibly to rebuild your credit history.

4. Monitor Progress:
   - Use credit monitoring services to track improvements and get alerts for changes to your report.

Step 4: Form Your Business Entity

If you're ready to start a business, set up your LLC to establish credibility and unlock access to business credit.

1. Choose a Business Name:
   - Verify the name's availability in your state.

2. Register Your LLC:
   - File the necessary paperwork with your state's Secretary of State office.

3. Get an EIN:
   - Apply for a free EIN on the IRS website.

4. Open a Business Bank Account:
   - Use this account exclusively for business transactions to maintain clear financial records.

Step 5: Apply for Business Credit

Once your LLC is in place, take steps to establish and grow your business credit profile:

1. Apply for a Business Credit Card:
   - Start with cards that cater to new businesses, especially those with introductory 0% APR offers.

2. Set Up Vendor Accounts:
   - Work with suppliers who report to business credit bureaus, such as those offering Net-30 terms.

3. Track and Manage Business Credit:
   - Keep utilization low and pay invoices on time to build a strong business credit profile.

Step 6: Launch or Scale Your Business

Use the knowledge and tools you've gained to turn your ideas into reality. Whether you're starting fresh or scaling an existing venture, these steps will guide you:

1. Invest Wisely:
   - Use business credit to fund essential expenses, such as inventory, equipment, or marketing.

2. Create a Marketing Plan:
   - Identify your target audience and focus on cost-effective strategies like social media, email campaigns, and SEO.

3. Track Your Finances:
   - Use accounting software to monitor income, expenses, and profits.

Step 7: Reinvest for Growth

As your business generates profits, reinvest them strategically to fuel long-term growth:

1. Expand Operations:
   - Use profits to hire staff, purchase new equipment, or explore additional markets.

2. Enhance Marketing:
   - Scale up successful campaigns to reach more customers.

3. Diversify Income Streams:
   - Launch new products or services to create multiple revenue sources.

Step 8: Commit to Lifelong Learning

The financial and business landscape is always evolving. Stay informed and continue developing your skills:

1. Read Books and Articles:
   - Explore resources on credit, entrepreneurship, and wealth building.

2. Attend Workshops and Webinars:
   - Learn from experts in your industry.

3. Network with Like-Minded Individuals:

   - Surround yourself with people who inspire and challenge you to grow.

Step 9: Share Your Knowledge

As you achieve success, pay it forward by helping others on their journey.

Share what you've learned with friends, family, or your community. Not only does this solidify your knowledge, but it also creates a ripple effect of empowerment.

Your Journey Starts Now

The journey to financial freedom and business success doesn't happen overnight, but every step you take brings you closer to your goals. By following the practical steps in this chapter, you're not just dreaming about success—you're actively creating it.

As you move forward, remember that challenges are part of the process. Stay disciplined, adapt to setbacks, and celebrate your progress. Your potential is limitless, and the tools you've gained in this book are your road map to unlocking it.

Let's keep building—your future is waiting.

9

Resources

Government and Consumer Protection Agencies

- Federal Trade Commission. (n.d.). Credit & loans. Retrieved from https://www.ftc.gov
- Consumer Financial Protection Bureau. (n.d.). Learn about credit reports and scores. Retrieved from https://www.consumerfinance.gov

Credit Bureaus

- Equifax. (n.d.). Understanding your credit score. Retrieved from https://www.equifax.com
- Experian. (n.d.). Improve your credit. Retrieved from https://www.experian.com
- TransUnion. (n.d.). Credit education. Retrieved from https://www.transunion.com

Educational Platforms

- MyFICO. (n.d.). Credit education center. Retrieved from https://www.myfico.com
- Credit Karma. (n.d.). Credit advice. Retrieved from https://www.creditkarma.com

Financial News Websites

- NerdWallet. (n.d.). Improve your credit score. Retrieved from https://www.nerdwallet.com
- Bankrate. (n.d.). Understanding credit scores. Retrieved from https://www.bankrate.com

Legal and Academic Sources

- Cornell Law School. (n.d.). Fair Credit Reporting Act (FCRA). Retrieved from https://www.law.cornell.edu
- Federal Reserve Bank. (n.d.). Reports on credit and lending. Retrieved from https://www.federalreserve.gov

Nonprofit Organizations

- National Foundation for Credit Counseling. (n.d.). Credit counseling resources. Retrieved from https://www.nfcc.org
- AnnualCreditReport.com. (n.d.). Free credit reports. Retrieved from https://www.annualcreditreport.com

Case Studies and Personal Stories

- Reddit Personal Finance Community. (n.d.). Real-life credit repair success stories. Retrieved from https://www.reddit.com/r/personalfinance

- Author's personal journey in improving credit (unpublished personal communication).

10

Conclusion

A s you've seen throughout this book, leveraging credit is far more than a financial tool—it's a gateway to endless opportunities. My journey, from building a 784 credit score at 22 to securing over $50,000 in business funding, wasn't about luck or privilege. It was about learning the system, applying the right strategies, and staying disciplined. If I can do it, so can you.

Credit has the power to transform lives. It gave me the resources to launch multiple ventures, help my mom start her own business, and build a foundation for long-term financial freedom. It allowed me to turn ideas into action, challenges into opportunities, and dreams into reality. But this transformation didn't happen overnight—it required persistence, careful planning, and a willingness to step outside my comfort zone.

Now, you're equipped with the same tools that changed my life. You've learned how to build and repair credit, form a business entity, secure funding, and reinvest profits to scale your ventures. But the most important lesson is this: action is what makes the difference. Knowledge alone won't unlock your potential; it's what you do with it that counts.

So, where do you go from here? Start by taking one step—whether it's reviewing your credit report, setting up your LLC, or applying for your first business credit card. Small, consistent actions will compound over time, leading to significant results. Trust the process, stay focused, and celebrate each milestone along the way.

Remember, credit isn't just about the numbers on a report. It's about what those numbers can unlock for you: the ability to build wealth, support your family, create opportunities, and leave a lasting legacy. The possibilities are limitless when you approach credit as a tool for growth rather than just a means to an end.

As you embark on this journey, I encourage you to dream big and believe in your potential. The road ahead may not always be easy, but it will be worth it. You have the power to rewrite your financial story and achieve goals you once thought were out of reach.

This isn't the end of your journey—it's just the beginning. The next chapter is yours to write. Go out there and unlock your future. You've got this.